THE HUMAN BODY:
The Skeleton

THE HUMAN BODY:
The Skeleton

Written and illustrated
by Kathleen Elgin

FRANKLIN WATTS | NEW YORK | LONDON

7   8   9   10

SBN 531-01180-1
Library of Congress Catalog Card Number: 74-152741
Copyright © 1971 by Franklin Watts, Inc.
Printed in the United States of America

THE HUMAN BODY:
The Skeleton

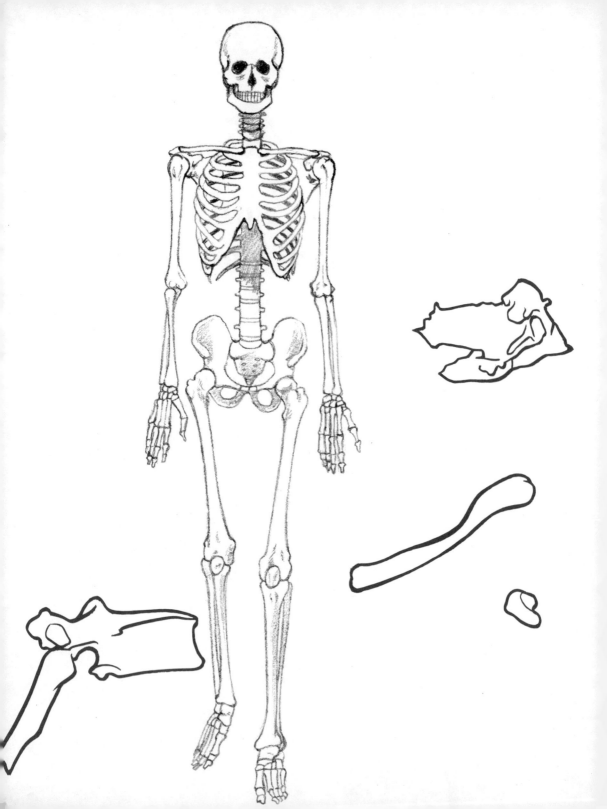

Your skeleton is your foundation and your
    framework. Its two hundred and six bones
    of various sizes and shapes are the support
    for your body.
The formation of these strong bones gives
    you your shape. Your head, neck, arms,
    legs, and backbone give you your human
    form. And the bones of the skeleton help
    protect the soft inner parts of your body.

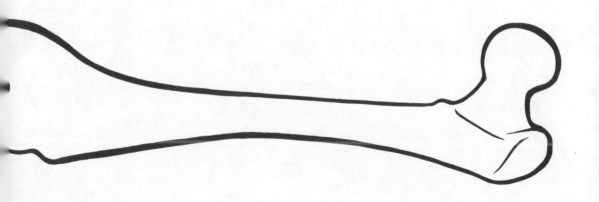

Your bones lock solidly together to form
  your skeleton. But if they locked too
  tightly you would not be able to move.
Bend over and touch your fingers to the
  ground. Feel your spine bend. It is made
  up of small bones connected by tough
  fiber and an elastic material called
  cartilage (CAR-ti-lij).
Some of your other bones are connected by
  cartilage, too. This material can stretch,
  and so helps keep your skeleton movable.

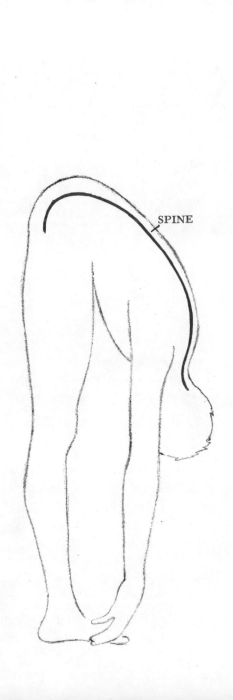

SPINE

CARTILAGE

11

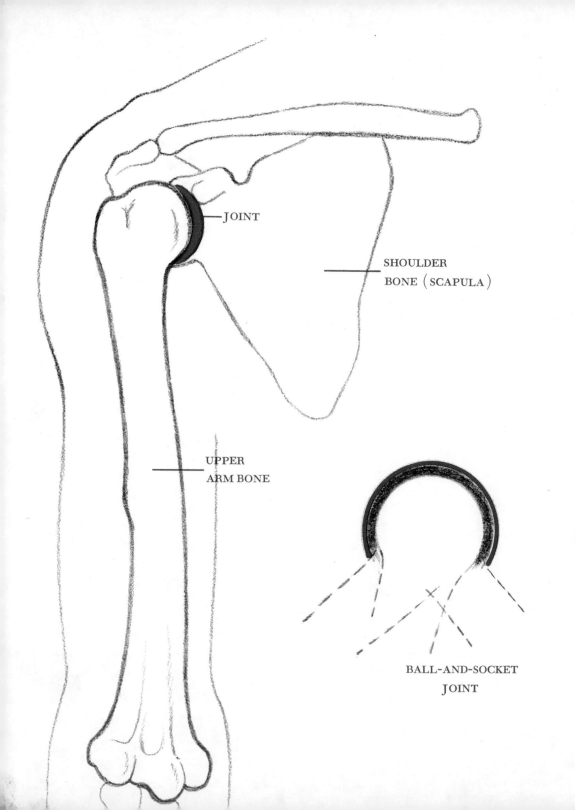

JOINT

SHOULDER
BONE (SCAPULA)

UPPER
ARM BONE

BALL-AND-SOCKET
JOINT

Wave your right arm in a circle while you
put your left hand on your right shoulder.
You can feel your shoulder move. There is a
joint there. It is called a *ball-and-socket*
joint.
The rounded end of your upper arm bone
fits like a ball into the socket of your
shoulder bone. Your fist can fit into the
cupped palm of your other hand in much
the same way. Try it.
The ball can roll in the socket. This action
in your shoulder makes it possible for you
to move your arm.

Still other bones are connected by a
  different kind of joint — a *hinge* joint.
  Hinge joints can bend somewhat like
  hinges.
Bones themselves cannot bend. They provide
  the rigid strength of your skeleton. For
  example, you cannot bend your forearm
  except at the wrist and the elbow, where
  there are hinge joints.

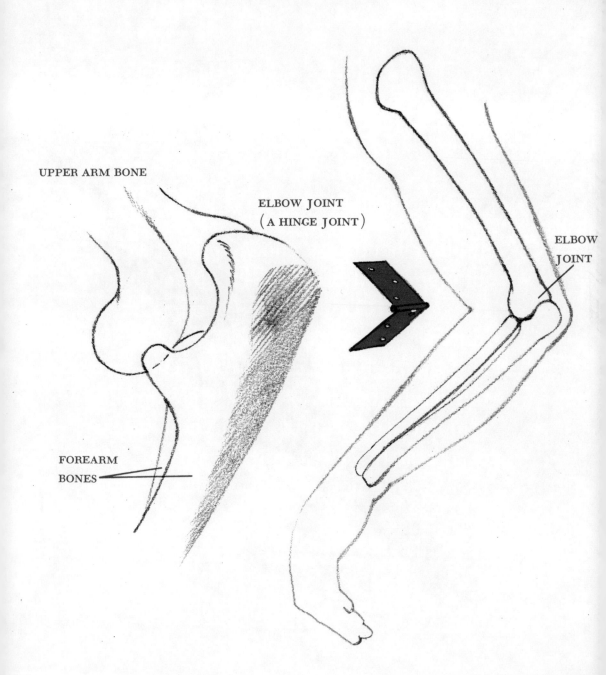

UPPER ARM BONE

ELBOW JOINT
(A HINGE JOINT)

ELBOW
JOINT

FOREARM
BONES

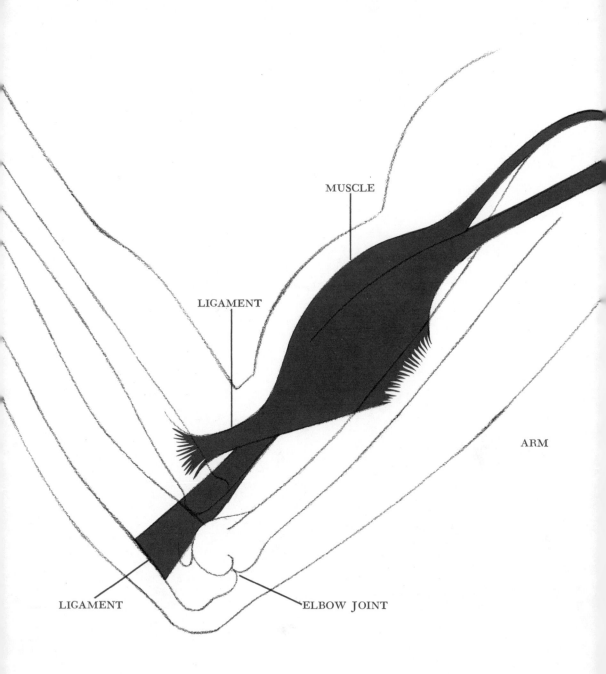

MUSCLE

LIGAMENT

ARM

LIGAMENT

ELBOW JOINT

16.

Strong bands called *ligaments* connect the
bones and support the joints. Ligaments
control the motion of the joints.

Although muscle is not part of your skeleton,
you could not move your bones if you did
not have muscles, too. They are fastened
to your bones. When the muscles tighten
or relax, the bones follow their motion.

Your bones have to be strong, but if they
were very heavy you could not move
easily. Bones are made of calcium,
phosphorus, other minerals, and a protein
fiber called collagen. The minerals and the
collagen are cemented together to make
bones light.
Yet the bones are strong and rigid enough
to bear your weight and all the extra
strains your body has to meet.

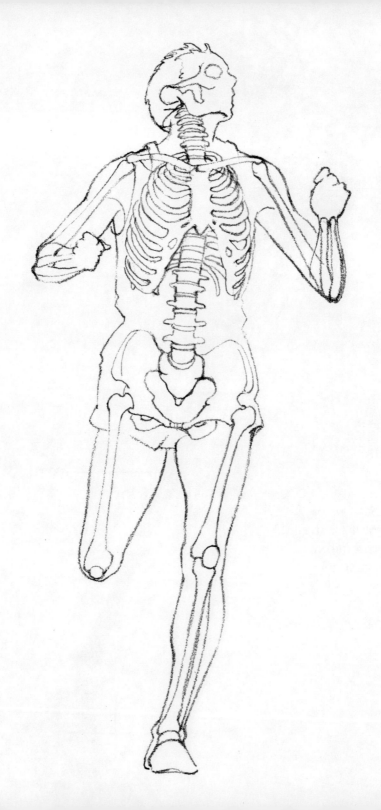

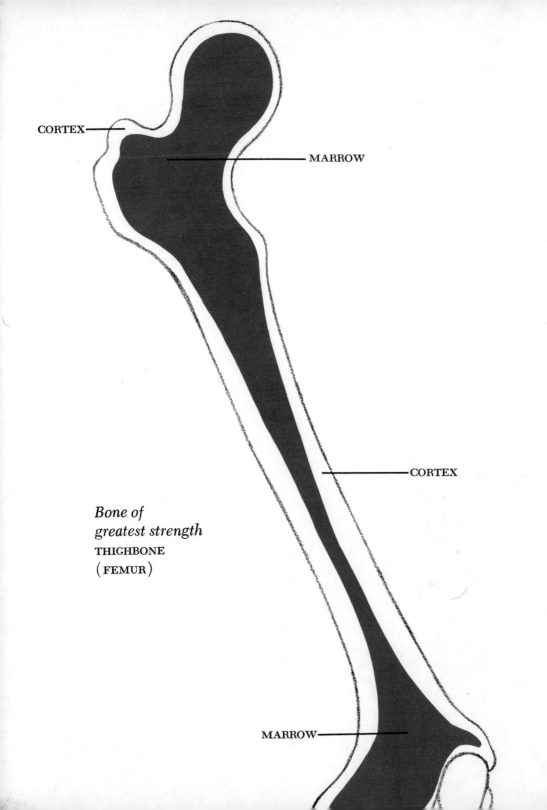

CORTEX

MARROW

CORTEX

*Bone of
greatest strength*
THIGHBONE
(FEMUR)

MARROW

All bones have an outer layer and an inner layer. The outer layer, the *cortex*, is firm. The inside of the bone is spongy, with a network of small, hard crystals. Among them, soft *marrow* is interlaced. In the marrow, the red blood cells for the body are made.

The outer and inner bone layers vary greatly in size and proportion. The bones that need the greatest strength have the heaviest cortex.

The cortex is covered by a tough shell called the *periosteum* (per-ee-OS-tee-um). The muscles and ligaments are attached to the periosteum.

Although the cortex of the bone looks solid, like ivory, it has many tiny blood vessels. Like other parts of your body, bone is living material.

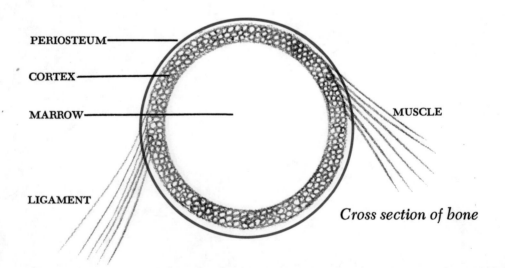

PERIOSTEUM

CORTEX

MARROW

MUSCLE

LIGAMENT

Cross section of bone

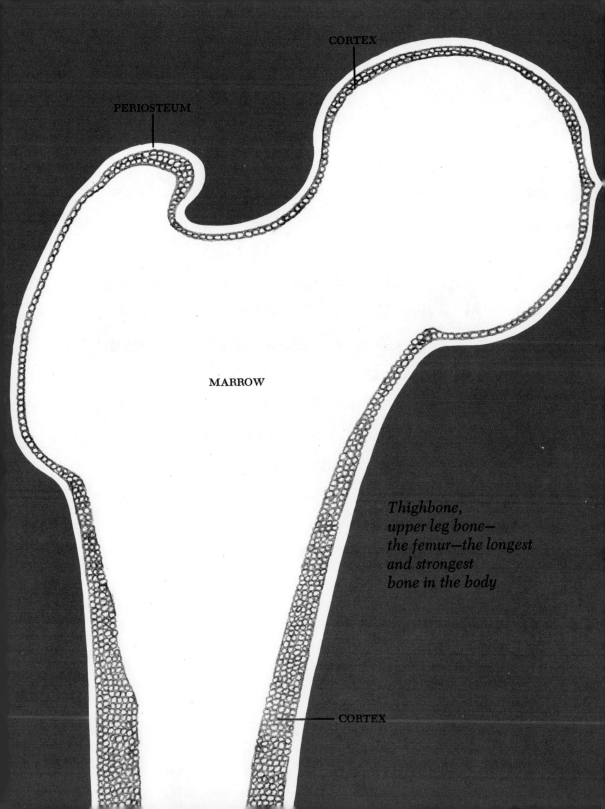

CORTEX

PERIOSTEUM

MARROW

Thighbone,
upper leg bone—
the femur—the longest
and strongest
bone in the body

CORTEX

As you grow taller and bigger your bones grow, too. They grow thicker by putting on extra layers. They grow longer by putting on cartilage in the sections just before their ends.

This cartilage grows and gradually changes to bone, until you have reached full size, when your bones are fully grown.

Even then, bone can grow new tissue. When a bone is broken, new-grown bone material heals the fracture.

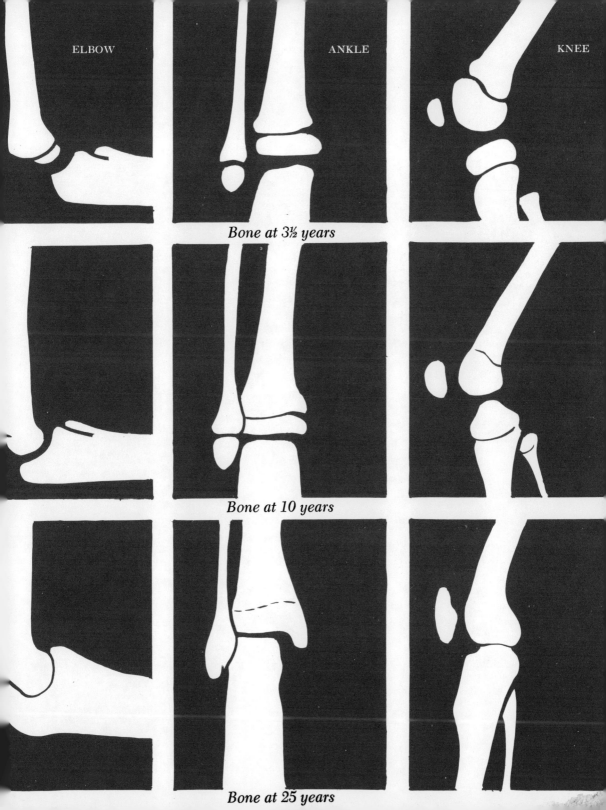

ELBOW   ANKLE   KNEE

Bone at 3½ years

Bone at 10 years

Bone at 25 years

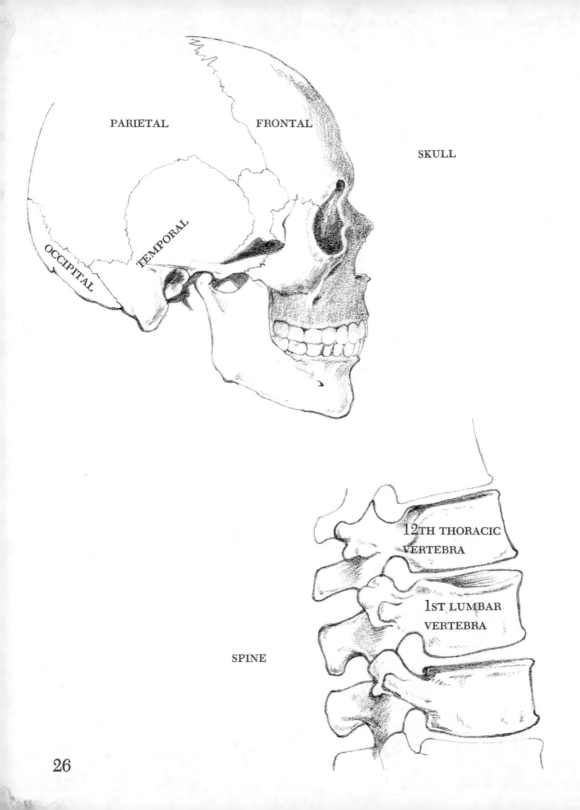

PARIETAL

FRONTAL

SKULL

OCCIPITAL

TEMPORAL

12TH THORACIC
VERTEBRA

1ST LUMBAR
VERTEBRA

SPINE

26

Some bones cannot move. The flat bones of
the skull are like this.
Some bones can move only in certain limited
ways. The parts of the spine are like this.
Some bones can move quite freely. Your
arms and fingers are like this.

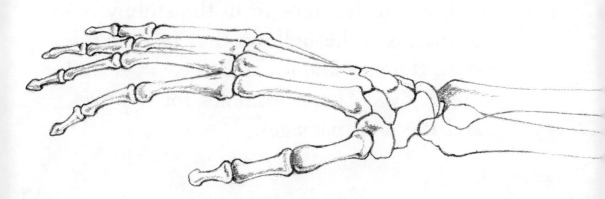

FINGERS, WRIST, AND ARM

At the top of the skeleton is the *skull*, the framework for the head. The shape of the skull is familiar to almost everyone. It looks rather solid, but it is made of twenty-two bones.

Eight strong, slightly curved bones make a protective box for the brain. Other skull bones protect the organs of hearing, sight, taste, and smell — your ears, eyes, mouth, and nose.

The bones of the face form the stubby base of the nose; the hollows that protect the eyes; the cheekbones; and the upper and lower jaws. There are holes for the eyes and the nose passages.

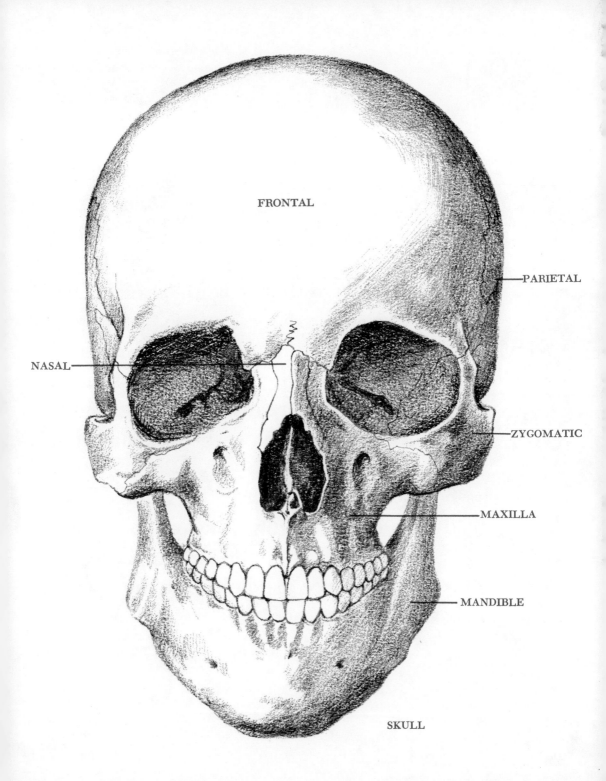

FRONTAL

PARIETAL

NASAL

ZYGOMATIC

MAXILLA

MANDIBLE

SKULL

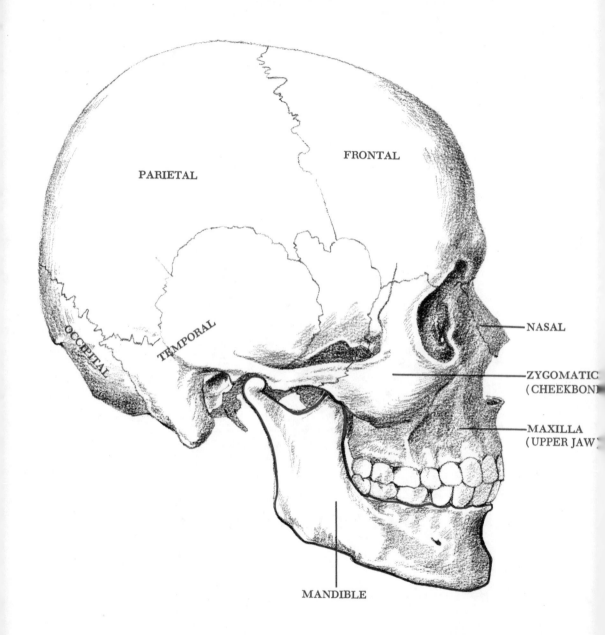

PARIETAL

FRONTAL

OCCIPITAL

TEMPORAL

NASAL

ZYGOMATIC
(CHEEKBONE)

MAXILLA
(UPPER JAW)

MANDIBLE

SKULL

The only part of the skull that can move is the *mandible* (MAN-di-bul), the lower jawbone.

The mandible has two joints that can move up and down. The joints can also rotate a little from side to side. This motion is necessary for chewing food.

The mandible's joints are on each side of the jawbone, just in front of the ears, between the mandible and the cheekbone and upper jawbone.

As in many other joints, the ends of the mandible's bones are made of cartilage. Over the surface of the cartilage is a layer of tissue. This tissue is kept moist by an oily fluid that lubricates the joints and makes them move more easily.

The teeth are also part of the skeleton. Their roots are sunk in the jawbones and are held there by the gums. The teeth are attached to the gums by a kind of calcium cement.

The center of each tooth is a pulpy core, which contains blood vessels and nerves. This center tissue is covered by *dentin*, which is rich in calcium. Dentin makes up the largest part of a tooth.

The part of the tooth that you can see, the *crown*, is protected by the hardest substance in the body. This substance is *enamel*. It can take tremendous pressures. It must be able to, for the body does not repair or replace enamel as it does material in other bones.

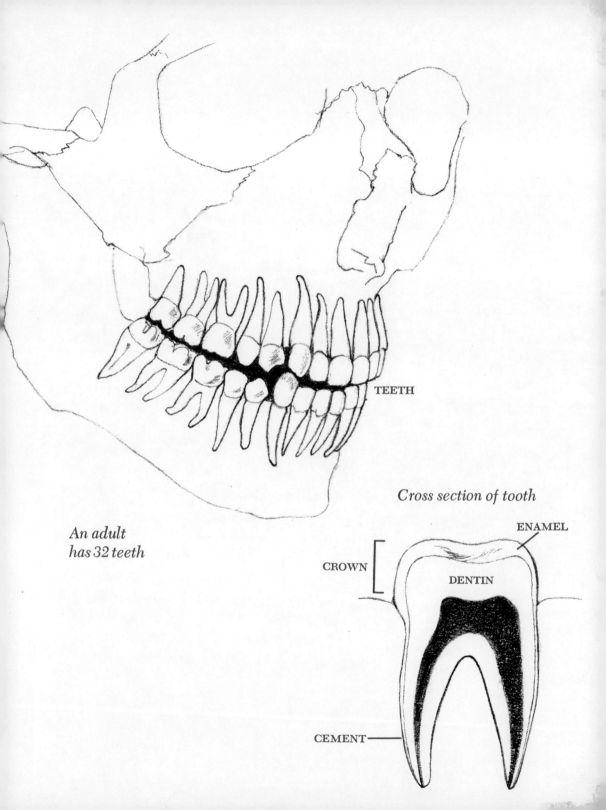

TEETH

*An adult
has 32 teeth*

Cross section of tooth

ENAMEL

CROWN

DENTIN

CEMENT

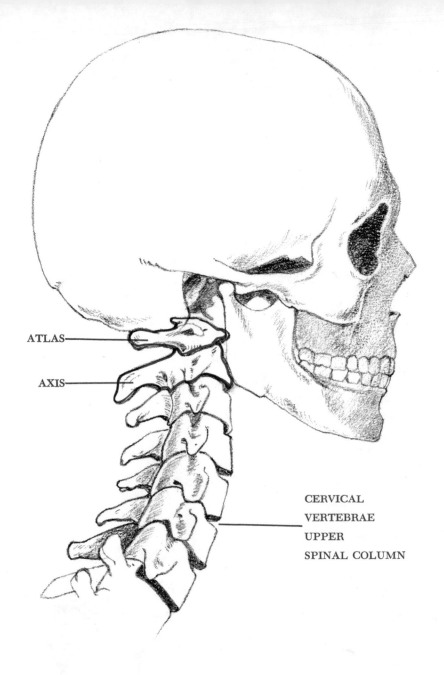

ATLAS

AXIS

CERVICAL
VERTEBRAE
UPPER
SPINAL COLUMN

The skull sits upon the *cervical vertebrae* (SER-vi-kal VER-te-bree), which are the seven bones of the neck. These bones form the top of the *spinal column,* or *backbone.*

The skull can move smoothly, in a semi-circular motion, up and down and from side to side, thanks to the two uppermost vertebrae in the neck.

The top vertebra holds the skull. This vertebra is called the *atlas,* for the Titan in Greek myths who was said to carry the world on his shoulders.

The second vertebra is called the *axis.* It can move like a pivot, on which both the skull and the atlas can turn.

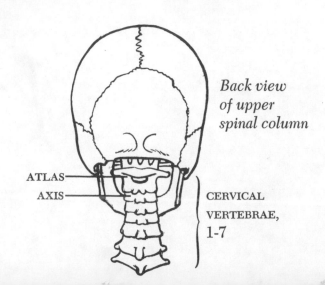

Back view of upper spinal column

ATLAS

AXIS

CERVICAL VERTEBRAE, 1-7

Next below come the twelve *thoracic*
(tho-RAS-ik) vertebrae, to which the ribs
are attached.

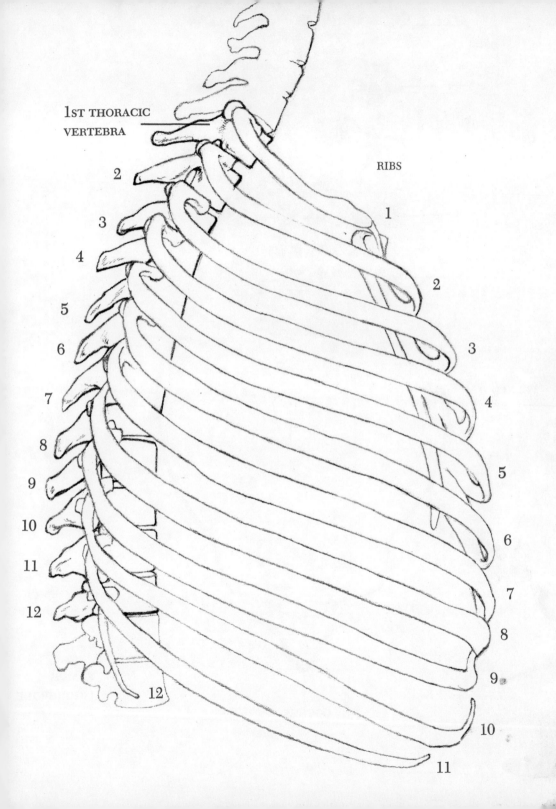

1ST THORACIC
VERTEBRA

2

3

4

5

6

7

8

9

10

11

12

RIBS

1

2

3

4

5

6

7

8

9

10

11

12

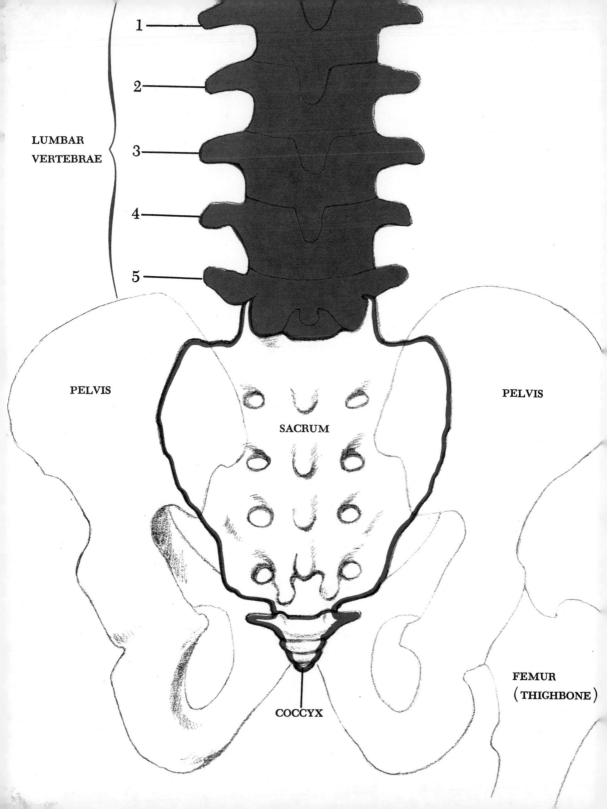

The five *lumbar* vertebrae complete the
number of movable vertebrae in the spinal
column.

The *sacrum* (SAK-rum) is formed of five
pieces of vertebrae fused together.

The *coccyx* (KOK-siks) is formed of four
pieces fused together.

The spinal column is vertical, but it has
gentle curves from front to back.
The twenty-four top, movable vertebrae are
pretty much alike. Each of these
vertebrae is somewhat like a ring. Through
the opening of the rings the spinal cord of
nerve tissue threads.

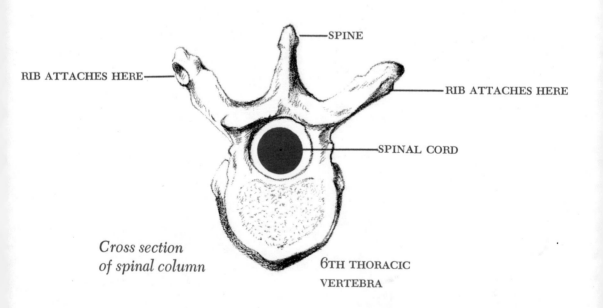

SPINE

RIB ATTACHES HERE

RIB ATTACHES HERE

SPINAL CORD

Cross section
of spinal column

6TH THORACIC
VERTEBRA

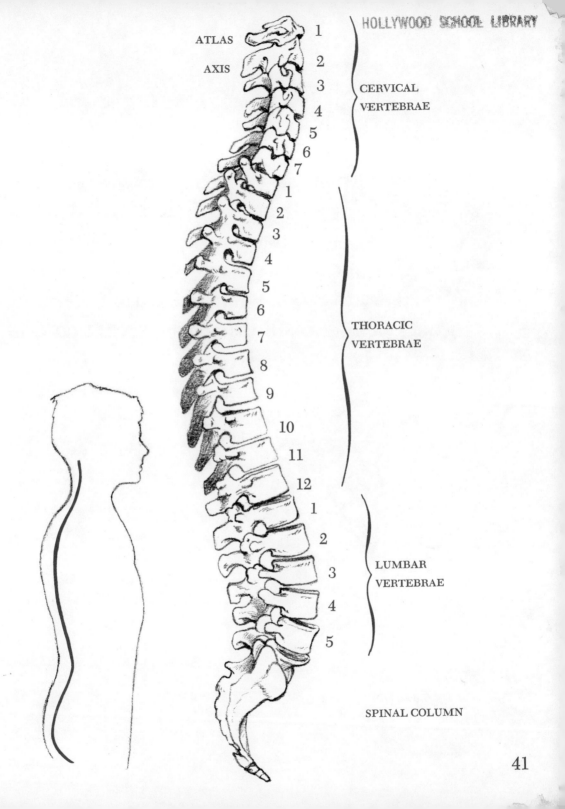

ATLAS

AXIS

CERVICAL
VERTEBRAE

1
2
3
4
5
6
7

THORACIC
VERTEBRAE

1
2
3
4
5
6
7
8
9
10
11
12

LUMBAR
VERTEBRAE

1
2
3
4
5

SPINAL COLUMN

41

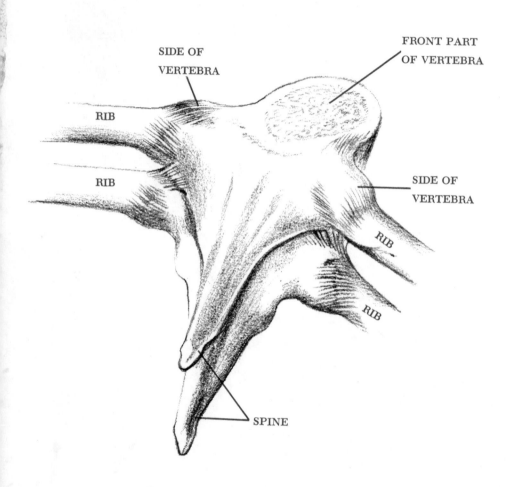

SIDE OF
VERTEBRA

FRONT PART
OF VERTEBRA

RIB

RIB

SIDE OF
VERTEBRA

RIB

RIB

SPINE

Section of vertebrae and ribs

The front parts of the vertebrae are very
heavy and give great strength to the spinal
column.
The sides of the vertebrae are formed by
winglike extensions reaching outward.
The backs of the vertebrae are the bony
parts you can see under your skin and can
feel with your fingers.
Some of the vertebrae's sharp projections join
with the ribs. They also anchor the
muscles of the back.

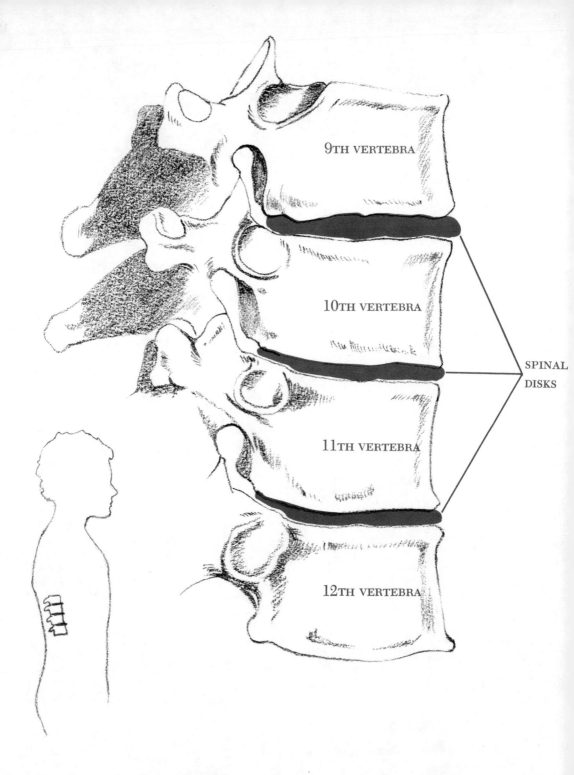

9TH VERTEBRA

10TH VERTEBRA

SPINAL
DISKS

11TH VERTEBRA

12TH VERTEBRA

Between each of the spinal vertebrae is the
spongy but tough cushion of cartilage and
fiber called a *disk*.
The disks let the bony vertebrae move freely
and smoothly, and keep them from
grinding together.
The disks are also shock absorbers. When
you sit down hard or walk on a pavement,
a jarring vibration starts running up your
spine. The spongy disks absorb this jarring.

In the back of the *rib cage* are the thoracic vertebrae. In the front of the rib cage is the *sternum* (STER-num), or breastbone. The twelve pairs of ribs curve around between them. But only the top seven pairs of ribs are connected directly with both the vertebrae and the breastbone.

Little pieces of cartilage join the breastbone ribs to the bone they meet. The elastic cartilage stretches every time you breathe and your chest expands. In this way, the rigid bone in the rib cage can protect the heart and lungs; yet at the same time the cartilage makes the cage flexible enough for breathing.

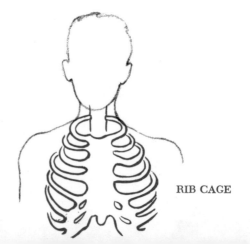

RIB CAGE

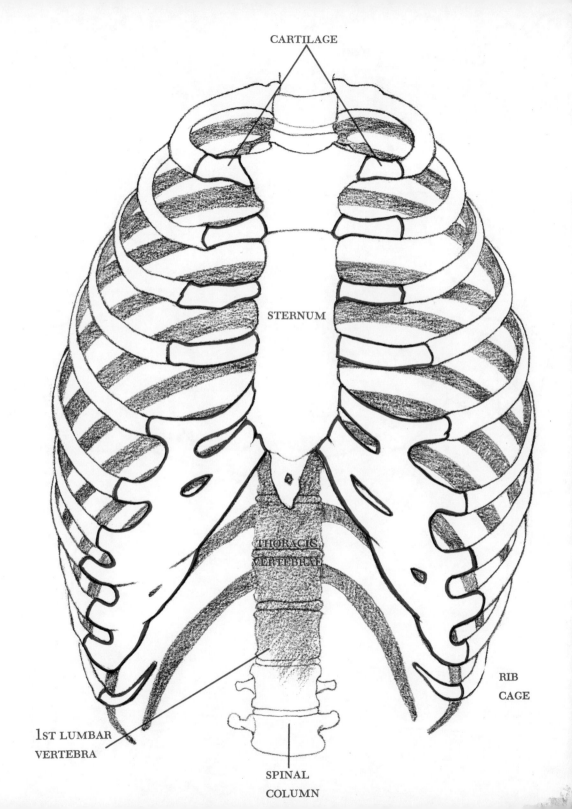

CARTILAGE

STERNUM

THORACIC
VERTEBRAE

1ST LUMBAR
VERTEBRA

RIB
CAGE

SPINAL
COLUMN

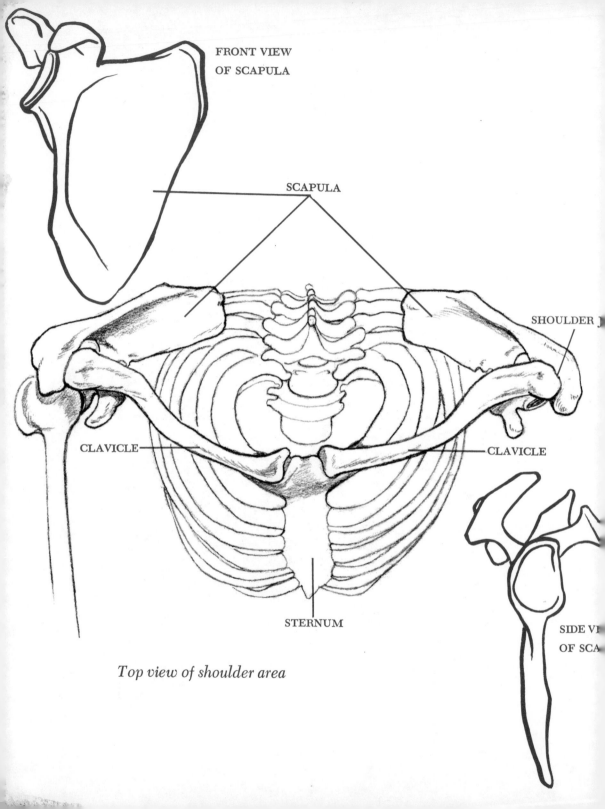

FRONT VIEW
OF SCAPULA

SCAPULA

SHOULDER J

CLAVICLE

CLAVICLE

STERNUM

SIDE VI
OF SCA

Top view of shoulder area

The shoulder area is formed by the *scapula* (SKAP-yoo-la), or shoulder blade, in back, and the narrow, curving bone called the *clavicle* (KLAV-i-kul), or collarbone, in front. If you are thin, you can see your clavicle across the top of your chest.

The clavicle is joined to the breastbone and to an overhanging ledge on the scapula.

The scapula is not attached directly to bone. It moves along with the arm, with which it forms a joint. This joint has a wider range of movement than any other part of the body.

Three long bones form the arm. The bone of the upper arm is called the *humerus* (HYOO-me-rus). It is one of the strongest bones in the body. Its rounded head fits into a socket in the scapula

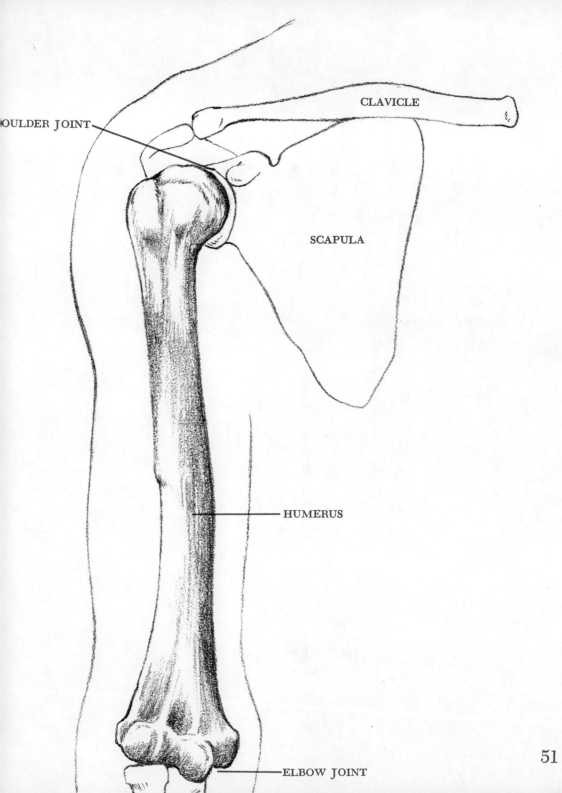

SHOULDER JOINT

CLAVICLE

SCAPULA

HUMERUS

ELBOW JOINT

51

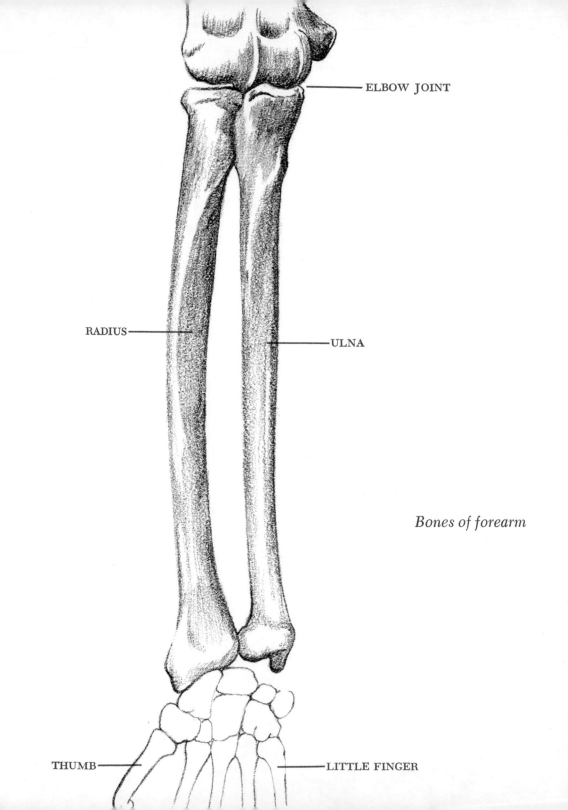

ELBOW JOINT

RADIUS

ULNA

Bones of forearm

THUMB

LITTLE FINGER

The elbow joint is a hinge joint. This joint
connects the humerus with the bones of
the lower arm, the *radius* (RAY-dee-us)
and the *ulna* (ULL-na). The radius is on
the thumb side of the hand. The ulna is on
the little-finger side.

The radius and the ulna can partially roll
back and forth over each other. This
rolling motion makes it possible for you to
turn your hand with the palm facing
upward or downward.

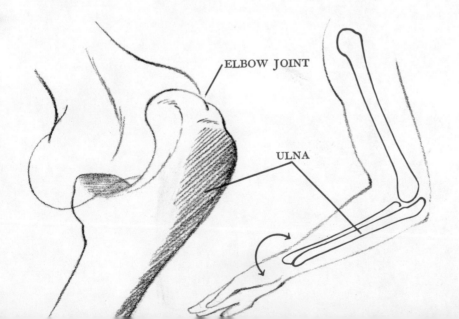

ELBOW JOINT

ULNA

There are twenty-seven bones in each hand and its fingers. These bones are small and delicate and are of various shapes.

There is a hinge joint at the wrist, and there are three joints in each finger and two in each thumb. These joints make it possible for you to bend your thumb and fingers and use your hand in many ways.

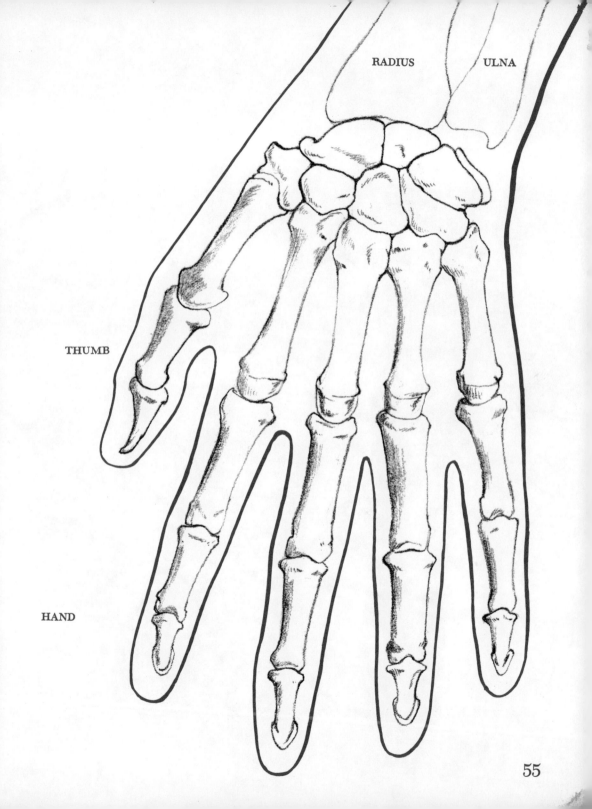

RADIUS

ULNA

THUMB

HAND

55

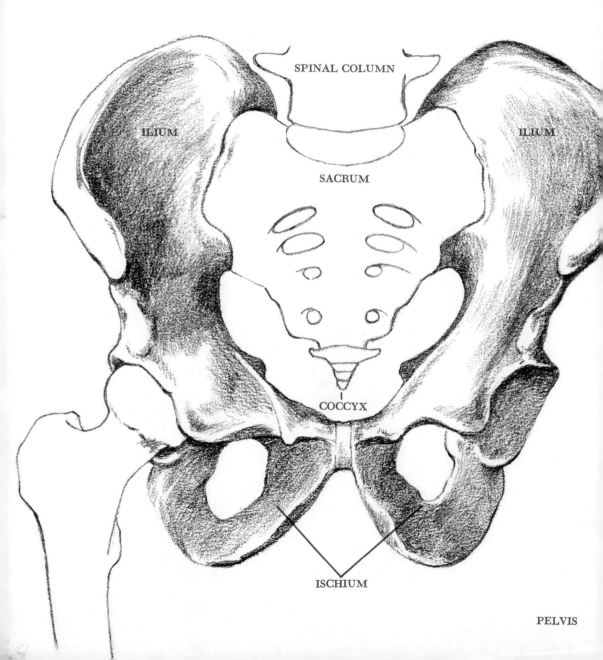

SPINAL COLUMN

ILIUM

ILIUM

SACRUM

COCCYX

ISCHIUM

PELVIS

The *pelvis* (PEL-vis), or hipbone, is a very
strong part of your framework. It goes
across your body at the lower part of your
spine. The pelvis is shaped somewhat like
a bowl. On it the upper part of your body
rests. From it your legs extend. It is
practically rigid. It needs to be firm rather
than flexible.

On each side of the body a fan-shaped,
curving pelvic bone called the *ilium*
(ILL-ee-um) flares out. The ilia are the
largest bones of the pelvis. In back, each
of them is attached to the sacrum.

Below each ilium the form of the pelvis is
completed by the *ischium* (ISK-ee-um)
bone.

From the ilia curve two *pubic* (PYOO-bik) bones, which are connected in front by a fibrous joint.

From each hipbone, a *femur* (FEE-mur), or thighbone, goes downward. The thighbones are the largest and heaviest bones of the body. They have to bear a good deal of bulk and weight.

The rounded top end of each femur fits into a socket on the hipbone. The movable, rotating joint that is formed makes it possible for you to kick and run and cross your legs and walk sideways as well as backward and forward.

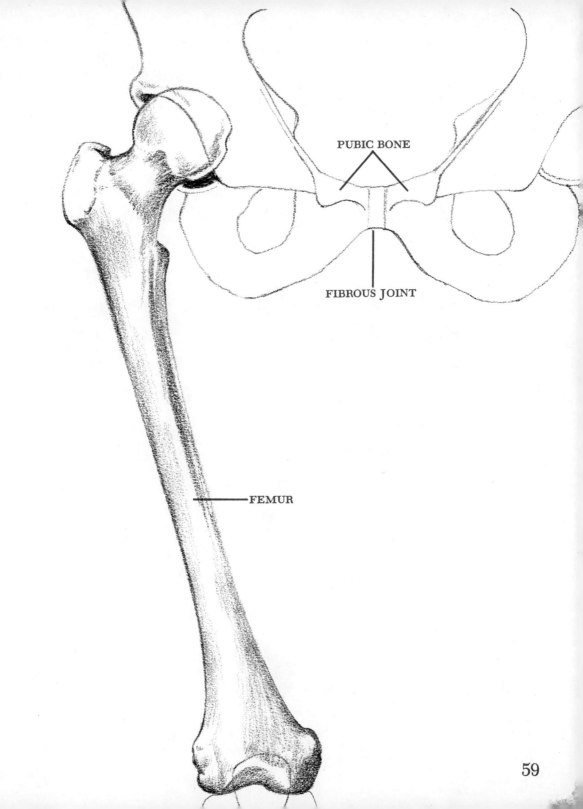

PUBIC BONE

FIBROUS JOINT

FEMUR

The lower end of the femur joins with the
lower leg at the hinged *knee joint*. If you
will bend your knee, you can see how this
joint works — and why it is called a hinge
joint.

Directly in front of the knee joint is a
rounded bone — the *patella* (pa-TELL-a),
or kneecap — which you can easily feel. It
protects your knee joint.

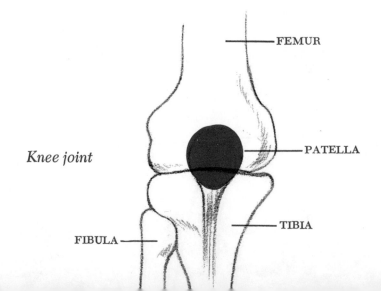

Knee joint

FEMUR

PATELLA

TIBIA

FIBULA

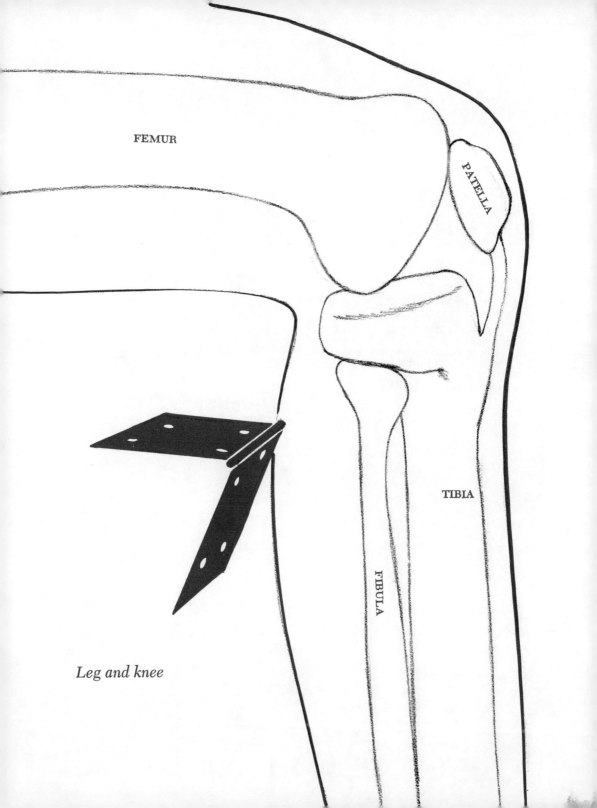

FEMUR

PATELLA

TIBIA

FIBULA

Leg and knee

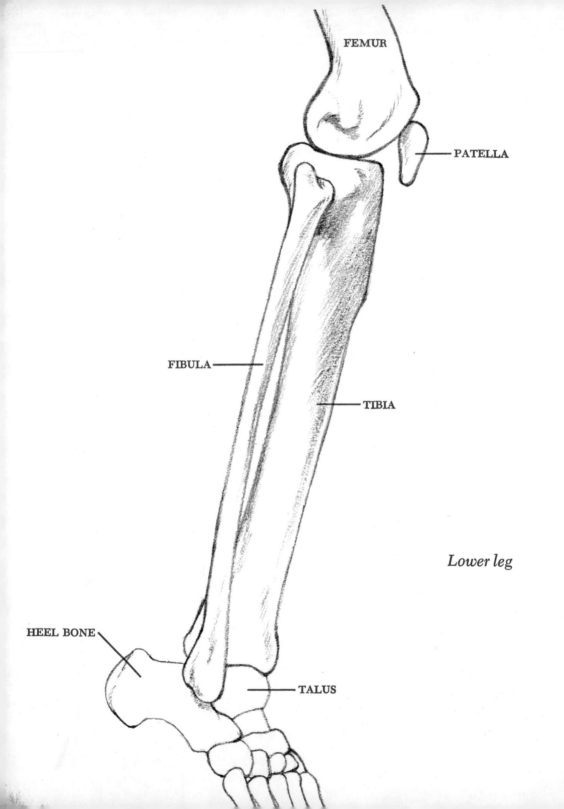

FEMUR

PATELLA

FIBULA

TIBIA

HEEL BONE

TALUS

Lower leg

The lower leg has two bones. The larger one is called the *tibia* (TIB-ee-a), or shinbone. The smaller one is called the *fibula* (FIB-yoo-la), or calf bone. The shinbone joins the knee. The calf bone is connected to the shinbone just below the knee.

The lower ends of the two bones of the lower leg meet the foot bone called the *talus* (TAY-lus), to make the hinged ankle joint. The ankle joint can turn and twist in various ways. When you walk, it bends to help give your foot a strong push forward. Try walking without bending your ankles.

There are twenty-six bones and thirty-two
joints in the foot. Some of the bones of
each foot lock together to form an arch.
This arch is strong. It is shaped so that it
can carry your weight without buckling.
The arch also keeps part of your foot off
the ground, so that you feel less shock
when you walk or run.
The joints of your toes work with your ankle
joints to push you forward when you
walk. Try walking without bending your
toes.

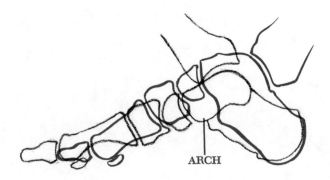

ARCH

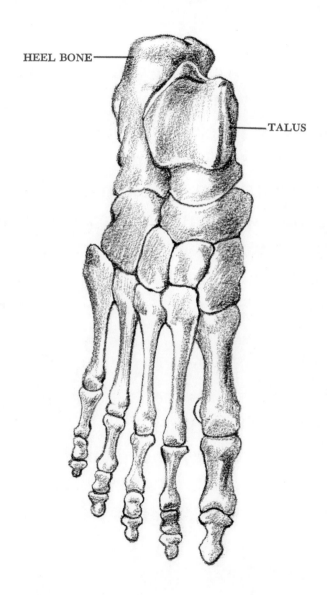

HEEL BONE

TALUS

Top of foot

Almost every bone in your body is designed
to fit a particular need.
Human beings can stand and walk on two
legs and use their arms in various ways
because of their skeletons.
The spine has gentle curves that help
humans to balance in a vertical position.
The feet are placed firmly on the ground.
The head is placed exactly right at the top
of the vertebrae.
The two symmetrical sides of the skeleton
help prevent the body from tipping in one
direction or another.
Joints and muscles and ligaments help the
bones to move.
The parts of the skeleton work together
almost miraculously.

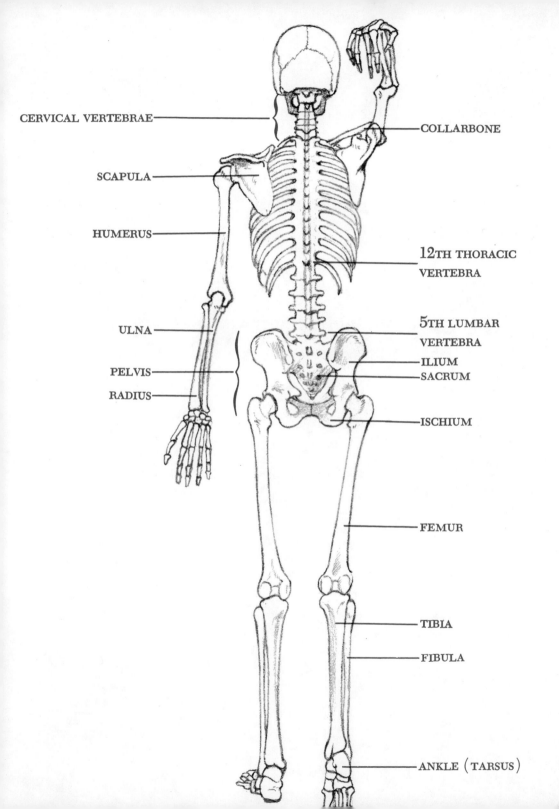

CERVICAL VERTEBRAE

COLLARBONE

SCAPULA

HUMERUS

12TH THORACIC
VERTEBRA

ULNA

5TH LUMBAR
VERTEBRA

ILIUM

PELVIS

SACRUM

RADIUS

ISCHIUM

FEMUR

TIBIA

FIBULA

ANKLE (TARSUS)

INDEX

Kathleen Elgin attended the Dayton (Ohio) Art Institute, and afterward worked in a stained-glass studio. There she executed a window depicting the history of medicine, for the Mayo Clinic.

In 1944, Miss Elgin came to New York to attend the American School of Design and to do free-lance work in advertising. By 1950, she was ready to begin illustrating books for young people. She has done this ever since and has to her credit a long list of titles, including the "Human Body" series, which she has both written and illustrated. In 1969, at the Children's Book Fair in Bologna, Italy, an international jury awarded the Graphic Prize for Children's Books to Miss Elgin for *The Heart*, a title in the "Human Body" series.